W.W.J.D.?

(What Would Jesus Do?)

A Drama For Today's Youth

Diane M. King

CSS Publishing Company, Inc., Lima, Ohio

W.W.J.D.? (WHAT WOULD JESUS DO?)

ISBN 0-7880-1353-X   PRINTED IN U.S.A.

To my parents and grandparents,
who first taught me about God's love
and who lived as a daily example
of that love on earth, and to the many lost souls
who keep wondering what's been missing in their lives.

Production Notes

Setting
The setting is purposely nondescript. This drama is designed to be easily adapted to any performance space, including sanctuaries and church gymnasiums.

Characters
Four main speaking parts:
  Stacy
  Jan
  Carmen
  Jean Beckman
Six minor parts:
  Four Friends
  Danny
  Darrell (non-speaking)
  Chorus of teen partygoers and homeless people at shelter

The characters are relatively nondescript. The actress playing Stacy must be able to portray a wide gamut of emotions. She should especially be able to bring across the subtle feelings she discovers as she progresses throughout the play.

Jan must be able to be "overly dramatic," especially when talking about Darrell in the beginning of Act I.

Carmen must be full of energy. At first she comes off as streetwise, fun, and a strong personality. It must be believable, however, for her to have the "soft side" that emerges later in the play.

Jean Beckman could easily be played by a pastor or youth leader if no teen can pull off the older character. She should be kind, gentle, and sincere.

Author's Note
Stacy could be changed to a male character. Jan, Carmen, and the girls could also be played as teen males with Darrell's role

being changed to a female. With a little creativity, the script can be easily changed to suit the performers available. This drama was designed to be easily adapted for any group of performers. The lines can be altered to suit the given actors of a particular performance. The messages are universal. Current teen slang, where appropriate, should be substituted for words that seem outdated. This script was meant primarily as a guideline on which to base your own unique production.

Other Notes

Bracelets can be anything the group decides. Youth groups could braid strings of craft cord and put four plastic or woodcraft beads on the braid. The letters "W.W.J.D." can be written on the beads with a permanent marker. For groups with limited resources, "W.W.J.D." can be written on people's wrists with a washable magic marker. For something special, a confirmation class could be given ID bracelets with W.W.J.D. engraved on them. The possibilities are endless. Much can be done with color to symbolize something personal to a group. People today seem to latch on to popular slogans, and teens are notorious for adorning themselves with various logos. Unfortunately, the cross, the traditional reminder of Christ, has been used so often in modern society without respect for its meaning that teens can become numb to its true meaning.

W.W.J.D.?

Act I

Any Town, USA; Any Place

(Stacy, a teenager, sits alone reading a book.)

Jan: *(entering)* Hi, Stacy. What's up?

Stacy: Oh ... Hi, Jan. Nothing. What's up with you?

Jan: Oh, you know ... same old — same old ... My parents are a major pain, I think school's a bore, shopping malls only carry what you want when you don't have any money, and of course ... *(pauses)* ... Darrell is the most fabulous, wonderful guy on Earth! *(grins and makes a big "lovesick" sigh)*

Stacy: Wow! Sounds like you and Darrell are really getting serious! How long have you two been together now?

Jan: It's been three perfect months. Oh, Stacy — I've never felt like this before ... I can't think about *anything* except Darrell.

Stacy: I can see that.

Jan: You don't understand ... when I'm away from him, I get this pain, like some sort of strange arthritis or something. I mean it actually hurts!

Stacy: And this is a good thing?

Jan: Sure! These crazy feelings I'm getting *must* be true love!

Stacy: Love? Are you sure?

Jan: Of course it's love! I mean, what else could it be? When Darrell and I are together I get this tingly sensation and things get all misty — like a dream — and then when we are close and he grabs me in his big, muscular arms and with our eyes meeting ... he holds my face ever so gently in his hands, presses his waiting lips against mine ... *(gets carried away thinking about Darrell)*

Stacy: *(interrupting)* All right! All right! I get the point. You think you are "in love" and Darrell is your dream come true.

Jan: Think it? I know it! I'm sorry ... I know I get carried away sometimes, but when I think about Darrell's eyes, his hair, his really, really cute smile, the way he ... *(starts to get carried away again)*

Stacy: *(interrupting again)* Jan! Jan! Hello? Earth to Jan! Anybody home in there?

Jan: Oh! *(giggles)* I'm sorry, Stacy, I guess I got carried away again. *(giggles again)*

Stacy: I guess. *(shrugs and goes back to her reading)*

Jan: *(after a pause)* So, when did you get back?

Stacy: Two weeks ago.

Jan: Two weeks ago! Why didn't you call me?

Stacy: I did. You weren't home.

Jan: Really? I wonder where I was?

Stacy: You were out with Darrell.

Jan: Oh ... um, sorry. I guess I should have checked my messages.

Stacy: I guess so.

Jan: *(after a pause)* Are you mad at me?

Stacy: No ... besides, I've been kind of busy, too.

Jan: Busy? Doing what?

Stacy: Do you really want to know?

Jan: I guess so.

Stacy: *(cautiously)* I've been busy helping my mom around the house, baby-sitting my little brother for free, reading the books we were assigned for summer reading from school, and reading the newspaper out loud at the nursing home on Main Street.

Jan: *(in disbelief)* Helping your mom? Baby-sitting for free? Reading to a bunch of senior citizens? Getting ready for school in the summer? *(jumps up dramatically)* Okay, you strange alien imposter! What happened this summer on that dairy farm up north? And what did you do with the *real* Stacy?

Stacy: Cut it out, Jan. It's no big deal or anything.

Jan: No big deal? Stacy, my best friend, the party girl of Jefferson Drive, goes away to her grandparents' dairy farm for three weeks and comes back acting like some sort of teenage Mother Teresa, and you think it's no big deal? C'mon, Stacy, what happened to you?

Stacy: *(uncomfortably)* It's nothing. Quit making a big deal over it, okay? It's just that, after I got back, I started to notice stuff I'd never really thought about before. Like how my mom needs help around the house. I mean, I noticed how tired and old she looks and how stressed she seems all the time. When I do stuff for her without being asked, she gets kind of surprised and seems a little happier — that's all. It just feels like the right thing to do, you know? Just like reading for school instead of waiting until the last minute. I guess I figured school was really the biggest responsibility in my life right now, and it just seemed right to put a little more effort into it than I did last year. I just decided that I might try to do ... you know ... the "right" thing for a while.

Jan: I don't know ... it still sounds pretty strange to hear you talk like this, Stacy. It's like you're a different person or something.

Stacy: I just had a lot of time to think while I was away ... Don't worry, Jan. I'm still the same person I always was, okay?

Jan: *(not believing her)* Okay, Stacy, if you say so ... *(after a long pause, continues excitedly)* SOOOOO, are you going to Carmen's big party Saturday night? She says it will be her best party yet!

Stacy: *(uncomfortably)* Um ... no ... I can't. I, uh, have something else to do.

Jan: *(stands there for a moment, jaw dropped open in disbelief. She composes herself and says flatly)* I see. *(mumbles to herself)* ... something else to do. Yeah, right. *(Jan stares at Stacy. This certainly was not the reaction Jan expected. She looks Stacy up and down, circling her, studying Stacy for any clues to her recent change.)*

Stacy: What? Stop it! Why are you staring at me like that?

Jan: Well, you look the same ... your hair, your face, your clothes ... I know something happened to you, Stacy, I just haven't figured out what it is yet. There has to be some sort of clue ... something to ... *(At this moment, Jan sees two, handmade bracelets on Stacy's arm. She screams.)* AAAAAHHHHHHH! OH, NO! This is it, isn't it? Oh, no! Oh, Stacy, Stacy, Stacy! *(reads)* "W.W.J.D." *(drops Stacy's arm and jumps back as if burned by it)* Oh, Stacy, you've joined some sort of weird dairy farmer cult, haven't you! *(begins*

10

to run away with the idea — building almost to hysteria as she considers each new possibility) Oh, man-o-man, Stacy, you're going to shave your head, start wearing beads and weird clothes. You're gonna change your name to "Sunshine" and start spending all your time in airports and bus stations passing out daisies and asking people about their karma, misting them with a spray of exotic incense that you hide in the folds of your long, flowing robe ...

Stacy: *(interrupting)* Jan ... Jan! ... JAN!!! *(Jan stops)* Stop it! Relax! ... Breathe! It's okay. I haven't joined some weird cult and I don't plan on shaving my head anytime soon. I wasn't exactly ready to try and explain all of this to anyone, but sit down and I'll try to do the best I can. Just promise me that you won't think I'm some sort of strange freak when I'm done, okay? *(Jan stops. She is shaken. Stacy continues.)* There's not much of a story ... You knew I wasn't very happy about being forced to spend three weeks of summer vacation stuck out in the middle of nowhere on a dairy farm, with only my eighty-year-old grandparents for company...?

Jan: *(nods, remembering)* I felt so sorry for you. Man! I bet you were miserable!

Stacy: I was at first. It was really different ... no rec center, no clubs, no big house parties like Carmen has. I was so bored when my grandparents were invited to a "barn raising party" and asked if I would go in their place, I was ready to go anywhere. *(pauses)* So, I went ...

Jan: Alone?

Stacy: Alone.

Jan: And?

Stacy: And it was wild! I mean, I can't believe my grandparents were invited to a party like that!

Jan: What do you mean?

Stacy: I mean that, in some ways, it was wilder than any party Carmen's ever had.

Jan: Oh, wow! Tell me more!

Stacy: Well, some people were acting crazy — drinking — you know, other stuff too. People were doing just about everything you could possibly imagine — pretty much right out in the open! I walked in the door and one guy passes me this big jug of wine and some other guy asks me to take a ride in his brand-new Corvette! I've never been to anything like it. Young people, old people ... all together doing whatever. And in the middle of all this, there's this one group of people who seem to be having the most fun of anyone ... and they're only drinking iced tea and coffee! It was really strange.

Jan: It sounds great! Here you are — miles from home — your grandparents' little grey heads tucked neatly in bed — on your own — with a party of a lifetime to experience. How lucky can you get? I'll bet you did it all, didn't you? I've seen you at parties before, Stacy-girl. I want to hear all about it, and don't leave out any of the juicy details. I want *lots* of details!

Stacy: That's just it. There's nothing to tell. Believe it or not, I didn't do anything. I drank iced tea, enjoyed the music, and was home before ten o'clock.

Jan: I don't get it. You had the perfect opportunity to do anything you wanted — *anything*. You could've stayed out all night long if you wanted to — in other words, a teenager's chance of a lifetime to experience *anything* you wanted, and you're trying to tell me you drank iced tea and turned in early?

Stacy: Yeah, that's about it. And you know what the really, really weird part was?

Jan: Don't tell me it gets weirder than this ...

Stacy: *(ignoring Jan)* I had the time of my life! I can't remember ever going out and having so much fun and feeling so great and full of energy when I got home. I didn't wake up with any regrets. I felt fantastic the next morning. And it was all because of this bracelet my grandmother gave me that made everything so different.

Jan: Stacy, you're scaring me. *First* you act like the Good Citizen of the Month, *then* you tell me this unbelievable story about the party, and *now* you're convinced your grandmother's making some kind of magical bracelets? Maybe you should see a doctor or something. My aunt knows at least two dozen therapists she swears have *all* helped her tremendously ...

Stacy: Look, Jan, I don't need a therapist, or shrink, or cult deprogrammer, or anything like that. The bracelet isn't magic, at least not really. I mean, it's just something she gave me and it started me thinking. And, even if I don't really understand it myself yet, I guess it *has* made some sort of a difference in me.

Jan: I don't get it. How can a homemade bracelet with somebody else's initials on it, "W.W.J.D.," make some big, profound difference in your life? Where did it come from anyway?

Stacy: My grandmother made it. The night of the "barn raising party" she gave it to me. I was asking her what time I had to be home. I figured she'd have some unreasonable, old-fashioned curfew for me.

Jan: What time did she say?

Stacy: She wouldn't answer me. I asked her a few times. I even tried to say it really loud in case her hearing might have been the problem. She never answered me. She just hands me this bracelet and makes me promise to wear it. I figured Grandma was, you know, starting to lose it a little bit and I didn't want to get her upset or anything, so I put it on and started to go.

Jan: Wow! What a great deal! No curfew — just wear this little bracelet and you get to set your own rules! Cool. Hey, Stacy, do you think you could get your grandmother to have a little talk with my parents?

Stacy: Yeah, I thought the same thing — that I was really getting away with something ... until I noticed the letters "W.W.J.D." stitched on top.

Jan: I wondered about that too.

Stacy: I was so excited to leave, I didn't notice the letters until I was almost out the door. I was in a pretty big hurry to go, but I was curious. Besides, I figured Grandma's answer might be pretty funny since she was acting so strange anyway.

Jan: Well? Did she tell you?

Stacy: She stood up, walked to the porch, kissed me on the check, and whispered in my ear, " 'What Would Jesus Do?' The letters 'W.W.J.D.' stand for the words 'What Would Jesus Do?' Please don't take it off." And then she says, "Have a good time tonight, Honey!"

Jan: And?

Stacy: And she shut the door. And then my ride came to take me to the party. It made me feel kind of uncomfortable at first. I've never exactly been the religious type or anything. I mean, I believe in God and all that, but, you know, it's not like I've got a "Honk For Jesus" bumper sticker on my car or anything.

Jan: Why didn't you just take the bracelet off?

Stacy: I thought about it. It's just that it seemed so important to my grandmother, and I sort of promised to wear it and, well, I just didn't feel right taking it off. Besides, I figured it wasn't really that big of a deal and what the heck — what difference could a stupid little bracelet make?

Jan: And?

Stacy: And I decided I'd go to the party, take advantage of my freedom, and have a night to remember.

Jan: So, what happened? How did you end up drinking iced tea and going home early?

Stacy: Remember when I told you some guy handed me a big jug of wine as soon as I walked in the door? *(Jan nods)* Well, I take it from him and just as I get ready to take a big swig of it, there it was, "W.W.J.D," "What Would Jesus Do?" an inch from my face, on my under-the-legal-drinking-age arm, tilting the biggest jug of wine I've ever seen to my lips. I don't know, I guess you might say the bracelet sort of "spoiled the moment." Anyway, I never did drink any wine or beer or anything stronger than iced tea. Funny, I realized I don't really like the taste of most of that stuff anyway, and the iced tea was the best I've ever tasted.

Jan: It's that easy?

Stacy: No, it's not easy. It just makes me feel good somehow to wear it, but I'm not sure I'm ready to tell the whole world about it yet. Some people aren't going to know how to take this.

Jan: Like people who jump to conclusions and assume you've joined some far out religious cult or something ...

Stacy: Yeah, something like that. I don't feel like I want to take the bracelet off, but I don't want everybody thinking I'm some sort of

15

outcast, religious fanatic or anything. The whole thing is kind of new to me. You're the first person I've told, Jan.

Jan: It's probably better that you don't tell everybody. You have to admit, Stacy, it takes some getting used to. It's a big change going from party girl to sainthood. It's a big jump.

Stacy: Slow down! I'm no saint or anything. I don't always do a very good job of following Jesus' example. I'm just saying that when I look at these bracelets it helps me make decisions and not feel so confused all the time.

Jan: Why two bracelets? Your grandma only gave you one on the night of the party, didn't she?

Stacy: She gave me the other one the last night I was there. She said it was in case I had a friend that needed it. You see, my grandma read this article in the paper about some other grandma somewhere who made these bracelets for her grandkids. The article said the kids liked them so much that they started wearing two, so they could give one to a friend. Grandma's Ladies of the Church group read the article and got so excited about it that they all started making these bracelets like crazy. In fact, she sent me home with a whole suitcase full of them. I guess she figured I had a lot of pretty messed up friends or something. I can't imagine giving them all away! Can you see me now? Pretty soon they'd start calling me "Bracelet Girl" and "Jesus Freak" and stuff like that. *(Jan laughs. Stacy scowls, shakes her head, and continues)* No. I'll just wear mine and, who knows, maybe some day I'll find some little kid who fell off his bike or something and I can give the other one away. I mean, none of our friends are really into church or religion or anything like that. I can't see giving one to any of them.

Jan: *(thinking — far away)* ... um ... yeah ... I guess you're right.

(Noise is heard from offstage)

16

Stacy: Hey, Jan, I don't know if I'm ready to talk about this to anyone else yet, so don't say anything about it, okay?

Jan: I won't.

(A group of girls enters. They are loud and boisterous and dressed to look tough and hard. They carry a loud, obnoxious boom box and are dancing and carrying on — showing off.)

Carmen: Stacy! My Party Girl! You're home! You poor girl! Shipped away for weeks to the middle of NOWHERE. You would not believe the major parties you've missed! I would never forgive my parents for being so cruel to me. I mean, you are soooo out of things, you know what I'm sayin', ladies? *(her friends giggle in agreement)* But first ... and *most* important.

Friend I: Definitely most important!

Friend II: Absolutely!

Friend III: It's going to be the best yet!

Friend IV: Yeah, you don't want to miss it!

Friend II: Everybody's going to be there!

Friend III: Carmen's parents are out of town again!

Friend I: Yeah, and her brother's coming home from college with a bunch of his friends.

Friend II: And we all know what that means, don't we, ladies?

(They all giggle.)

Friend IV: Yeah, good lookin' college men!

(They explode into laughter.)

Friend III: I'll bet there'll be all kinds of, you know, "college stuff" going on at the party.

Friend I: Yeah, and we'll be right in the middle of it!

(They all agree and start talking among themselves, excited about the party. Carmen is obviously pleased with all the anticipation.)

Carmen: Soooooo, Stacy — Jan — remember — Saturday night. You *don't* want to miss it. This is going to be the most important event Jefferson Drive has ever seen. Oh, and, Jan, because you are one of my personal best friends, I've made some "special arrangements" for you and Darrell Saturday night — if you know what I mean. *(The girls all giggle.)* So, you guys will be there?

Jan: Darrell's picking me up at eight.

Carmen: Perfect! My parents' plane leaves at six. The party should be going good by eight. How about you, Stacy? Eight o'clock okay for you, too?

Stacy: *(has been quiet so far and nervously fidgets with the bracelet on her arm)* Um .. I'm really sorry, Carmen, but I can't come Saturday night.

Carmen: Oh, don't worry about your mom. Sarah's older sister said she'd cover for us, so we all said we were spending the night at her house. We've got it all worked out.

Stacy: *(without enthusiasm)* Yeah, it sounds like it ... Look, Carmen, it's not my mom, it's just that I've got something else to do Saturday night — something I promised to do *before* I knew about your party.

18

Carmen: Aw, c'mon, Stacy. You can't get out of it? You've just got to be there, Party Girl! It won't be the same without you. You've missed so much already ... Please?

Stacy: I guess I probably could get out of it ... *(thinks about it — her hand unconsciously reaches for the bracelets)* No, Carmen ... I'm sorry, I made a promise ... I've got to go.

Carmen: I don't get it, Stacy. What could possibly be so important?

Stacy: You wouldn't understand, okay? It's just somewhere I promised I'd be and there are people counting on me to show up.

Carmen: Yeah, well we were counting on you too, Stacy. I can't believe you're ditching us for some other people. I thought we were friends.

Stacy: We *are* friends, Carmen. It's just that this is important.

Carmen: *(insulted)* Oh, and my party — the biggest party Jefferson Drive has ever seen — isn't important? Thanks a lot, Stacy. I see how it is. *(turns to leave)*

Stacy: Carmen! Wait! Carmen! Stop! *(She is frustrated and all at once her thoughts come spilling out.)* Look, Carmen, I'm spending Saturday night making food at the homeless shelter downtown and helping a lady named Jean Beckman feed it to a bunch of hungry, homeless people who won't get to eat if I break my promise and go to your party. And, yes, Carmen, I'm sorry, but I *do* think feeding a bunch of homeless people the only food they're probably going to get that day is somehow more important than going and having fun at a party — no matter how great the party is. So get off my back about it ... okay?

Carmen: Okay, okay! Calm down! I get it! I guess I'd feel guilty too if I had already promised someone. Too bad it had to be Saturday night. How did you meet this Jean Beckman lady anyway?

Stacy: *(quite frustrated. She hadn't planned to tell this much. She continues with a sense of defeat.)* I went to church Sunday with my mom, and Ms. Jean got up and told all about how she feeds these people every day, and how she needed help, and when she asked for volunteers, I really didn't have anything else to do, so I signed up. It's just that she's counting on me to be there. I'm sorry ... I hope you understand.

Carmen: I guess so.

Stacy: Then we're still friends?

Carmen: Still friends. *(they double high five — Carmen notices the bracelets.)* Hey! Cool bracelets! Wow! I love these colors, Stacy! One of these would look soooo good with my outfit for Saturday night. Let me have one, Stacy ... you have two of them. C'mon, Stacy, let me have one ... please? C'mon, please?

Stacy: Carmen, I don't think you really want to wear one of those ...

(Before Stacy can finish, Carmen is already taking the bracelet off of Stacy's arm and trying it on herself.)

Carmen: *(excited)* Oh, this is perfect! I really like it! Check it out! *(reads)* "W.W.J.D." Huh? I wonder what that's supposed to mean? It must be some new designer I've never heard of before. I know! "W.W.J.D." can stand for the Wild Women of Jefferson Drive. Hey! I like that! Check it out, ladies, "W.W.J.D." *(shows the bracelet to her friends)* Saturday night we're gonna be the Wild Women of Jefferson Drive.

(The girls start to dance and chant)

Girls: *(as they exit)* W.W.J.D. Wild Women of Jefferson Drive. That's you — that's me — on Saturday night that's who we'll be. W.W.J.D.

(They continue off. After Carmen and the girls dance out, Stacy sits and buries her face in her hands.)

Stacy: I can't believe it. *(shakes her head)* This is getting out of control. It's happening so fast.

Jan: What do you think Carmen will do when she finds out that "W.W.J.D." doesn't stand for the "Wild Women of Jefferson Drive"?

Stacy: I don't know. I'm hoping she'll never ask. *(touches the remaining bracelet. After a long pause, Stacy continues quietly)* Carmen said she made "special arrangements" for you and Darrell Saturday night. What did she mean by that?

Jan: *(quietly)* She means a room.

Stacy: A room?

Jan: Yeah, Stacy, a room. Oh, don't be so naive. *(turning away)* Carmen means she's reserved one of her bedrooms so Darrell and I can be alone Saturday night.

Stacy: Jan, you're not thinking of doing anything stupid, are you?

Jan: I don't know, yet. Anyway, what's so stupid about it? I love Darrell and he says he loves me too. Look, Stacy, lots of our friends are doing it. We know kids at school who are parents already. Besides, it's not like I've decided anything yet.

Stacy: You talk about *me* changing. You always said you were planning on waiting, you know, until you got older. It sounds like you're the one who changed, Jan. What happened to going to college, getting married, you know, all that stuff you used to talk about before you met Darrell?

Jan: I don't need you to tell me what to do, Stacy. I can make my own decisions, okay? Just because you suddenly "found God" doesn't mean you can start trying to make everybody else feel all guilty about being human.

Stacy: I wasn't trying to make you feel guilty. I was just trying to be a friend, okay?

Jan: Don't worry, Stacy. I know what I'm doing. Just leave me alone about it, okay? Just leave me alone!

Stacy: Okay.

Jan: *(after a long, uncomfortable pause)* Well ... um ... I've got to go. I'll see you later.

Stacy: Hey, Jan! Before you go ... here ... *(takes bracelet off her arm and starts to hand it to Jan)* Why don't you go ahead and take this? I didn't mean to upset you. I want you to have it.

Jan: Oh, I don't know, Stacy. I mean ... it's yours ... you *believe* in all that religion stuff now. I just don't think I should wear it.

Stacy: C'mon ... just take it ... call it a "peace offering" or a "friend-ship" bracelet — whatever you'd like, okay? You can pretend you're like Carmen and it means "Wild Women of Jefferson Drive."

Jan: That might work for Carmen, but I already know what it really means. I do believe in God and I think Jesus was a great guy and all, but like I told you before, I'm just not into all that religion stuff, Stacy.

Stacy: No one said you had to be. You said you were still making decisions about Darrell and since the whole idea behind the brace-let is to help people with decisions, I mean ... well ... it seems to help me, Jan. I'm just trying to help — that's all.

Jan: Well, I'm not you, Stacy! Some help. You're trying to make me feel guilty! You're trying to give me something that's going to come *between* me and Darrell. I don't want your help. You're not my friend! If you were really my friend, you would be happy for me, not trying to ruin my relationship with Darrell.

Stacy: I *am* your friend! I'm not trying to ruin your relationship with Darrell. I'm trying to help it!

Jan: Yeah, right! Look, I think I liked you better before you started thinking about God all the time. Just stay away from me, okay, Stacy? Just leave me alone!

(Jan leaves in tears.)

Stacy: Jan! Wait! Stop! I was just trying to help ... *(alone, to herself)* I was just trying to do what I thought Jesus would do. *(continues sarcastically)* Great job, Stacy. You've just lost your best friend. What else could go wrong?

(She takes off the bracelet, holding it in her hands. She turns it over looking at it, tracing the letters with her finger. She is lost in thought. Carmen calls from off right.)

Carmen: Stacy! Hey, Stacy, are you still here?

Stacy: *(looking up and speaking to the sky)* Please, don't make me do this.

Carmen: *(entering)* Hey, Stacy Girl! I'm glad you're still here. I just wanted to thank you for the bracelet. I love it! I've been showing it to everyone!

Stacy: *(without enthusiasm)* I'm glad you like it, Carmen.

Carmen: Yeah, it's great. But, you know, the more I looked at it the more I just had to know, what does "W.W.J.D." really stand for? I kind of got this funny feeling I wasn't exactly right with "Wild Women of Jefferson Drive." Was I?

Stacy: *(uncomfortably)* No, Carmen, that's not what the letters stand for.

Carmen: Well, that's what I figured. Anyway, I thought that if I was going to show it to everybody, I should probably know what I'm wearing ... you know, so I don't make a fool out of myself or anything.

Stacy: Why don't you just let it mean whatever you want it to and leave it at that?

Carmen: *(sensing Stacy's reluctance)* What's the big secret? It can't be *that* bad, can it?

Stacy: It's not bad ... Look, Carmen, you really don't want to know, okay?

Carmen: Look, Stacy, don't tell me what I want and don't want. Just tell me what it means, okay? *(stands waiting, making it clear that she is not leaving until Stacy answers her)*

Stacy: Okay, but you're going to take it wrong.

Carmen: I promise I won't "take it wrong." Just tell me, Stacy ... we're friends ... you can trust me.

Stacy: *(pauses, takes a deep breath and stares straight ahead and says quietly)* The letters "W.W.J.D." stand for "What Would Jesus Do?"

Carmen: *(saying each word slowly — confused)* What ... Would ... Jesus ... Do?

Stacy: *(upset — defeated — with a sigh)* Yes, Carmen: "What Would Jesus Do?"

Carmen: *(not listening. She is looking at her bracelet and tracing the letters with her finger. She seems faraway, lost in thought)* What Would Jesus Do? *(looks at Stacy as if she is a stranger)* Well, um ... uh ... I, uh, gotta go ... *(pauses)* I just wanted you to know ... I mean ... thanks for ... um ... you know ... um ... I'll catch you later, okay?

Stacy: *(miserably, without looking at Carmen)* Yeah, right ... sure ... catch you later ... I'll bet ... *(looks up to the sky. She addresses God)* Hello? God? Are you there? *(thinks about this for a moment, then says to herself, under her breath)* Duh, Stacy ... Of course, He's there ... He's God ... He's everywhere. *(addresses the sky again)* Uh ... God? I know I haven't talked to You a whole lot recently. I've really been meaning to get around to it. *(talks to herself again)* Oh, great, Stacy. Smart move ... try to tell God He's not very important! *(again to God)* Actually, that's why I'm talking to You now. You see, I think You've got the wrong person. I mean, I think You made a mistake ... yeah, that's it ... a mistake. No, wait a minute. You're God. You don't make mistakes. Okay ... *(struggles for her thoughts and, frustrated, blurts out)* Well! I hope You're happy! I mean, look at me! I am a complete wreck. I don't even know how to talk to You. I keep getting this feeling that You're trying to tell me something — that You're trying to lead me somewhere — but I don't know where that is. I mean, I wore the bracelet. I got the message ... isn't that enough? Can't we just keep this between You and me? Do we have to get everyone else involved? *(she is hopeful, nodding, looking up, almost waiting for an answer. She frowns)* No, I guess it's already too late for that now. I can't stand to think what Carmen and all her friends are saying about me now. I saw the way she looked at me. I bet she'll have great fun telling everyone at the party Saturday night how I'm a goody-goody little Christian who gave her a "Jesus Bracelet." *(winces, as if in pain, and continues)* And as if that wasn't enough ... this whole thing ... trying to think "What Would Jesus Do?" has made me lose my best friend. I didn't sign on for this, God. I'm not sure this is the best way to convince someone to follow You. I mean, let's look at the score here. Trying to think "What Would Jesus Do?" before I make

25

a decision has gotten me — what? I'm missing the biggest social event of the year — which, of course, I probably wouldn't be welcome at anyway because all of my friends think I'm now some sort of weird religious fanatic *and* my best friend, who probably needs me now more than ever before, won't even talk to me. And it all started because of this stupid bracelet! Why did Grandma have to give me this stupid thing, anyway? Why do I feel like I have to do the "right" thing when I wear it? Well, I'm tired of "doing the right thing." "Doing the right thing" is hard. It was like the more I started to think about You — the more You seemed to want from me. It's like You're pushing me down some sort of path as some sort of mean, cruel joke. You made Your point, okay? Wasn't it enough that I didn't drink the wine at the party — that I came home early? That I'm helping my mom? That I'm giving up my Saturday night to feed the homeless? You can see that I've changed. C'mon, God. It seems like the more I do, the more You expect me to do. Can't we strike some sort of a deal? How about ... say ... one act of faith a week? Would that be enough? Does trying to do what Jesus would do really have to change my whole life like this? It's like it's some sort of contagious "Jesus Disease" and You want *me* to be the carrier or something. Can't somebody follow Jesus' path without everybody knowing about it? Can't Christianity be a big secret? Besides, what good is it to try to give these bracelets away, anyway? Carmen has one bracelet because it matched her outfit, and Jan, my best friend, acted like the other one was poison and I was trying to kill her with it. Who am I trying to kid? This is too hard. I'm not cut out to be the "Voice of Morality" for the next generation. Look, I'm a failure at this. You've got the wrong person for the job ... *(begins to break down)* Why won't You tell me what I'm supposed to be doing? Why won't You help me? Why won't You answer me? If You could just give me some sort of a sign ... you know ... to let me know that You're listening ... to let me know that I'm on the right track. A clap of thunder, flash of lightning, burning bush, plague of locusts, anything ... just let me know that You're listening ... that any of this matters ... that I matter ... Answer me! *(getting angry)* Do you hear me? Answer me!

(looks to the sky and after a long, long pause, she continues, quietly, trembling) I didn't think so. Look, God, I'll go feed the homeless on Saturday night, but that's where it ends, okay? I'm done with this bracelet and all the others. I guess I'm just not cut out to live my life by "What Would Jesus Do?" You'll just have to find someone better to spread Your Word. Someone with more practice doing the right thing. I'm not the one ... I'm done ... I'm really done. *(With this Stacy looks up to the sky, takes the bracelet off, and drops it in front of her as an almost symbolic gesture. She looks at it on the ground for a minute and then picks up her book and hurries off.)*

Jan: *(from offstage, as she enters)* Stacy, I'm sorry I blew up like that before. I guess I'm under a lot of stress ... *(looks around)* Stacy? Stacy, are you here? *(sees the bracelet, picks it up, calls out)* Stacy, you forgot your ... *(fades out as she realizes no one can hear her. She looks at the bracelet, pauses to think for a moment, and carries it out.)*

Act II

The Homeless Shelter

(Ms. Jean and Stacy are passing out brown bag dinners to various homeless people.)

Jean: Well, we've had a good night. This is the last box. A lot of people were able to eat tonight. I really appreciate your help, Stacy. Thank you. *(hugs Stacy)*

Danny: *(takes a bag from Jean)* Thanks, Ms. Jean. I've been lookin' forward to this all day.

Jean: You're welcome, Danny. C'mere, let me give you a hug. *(hugs him and says in his ear)* God loves you, Danny, and I love you.

Danny: Thanks, Ms. Jean.

(Smiling, he turns and sits to eat. Ms. Jean busies herself with the bags.)

Stacy: Ms. Jean? May I ask you something?

Jean: Sure, honey, what is it?

Stacy: Why are you doing this? Why are you here like this every night? I mean, what do you get out of it? I thought that a lot of these homeless people were alcoholics and drug addicts who don't want to get sober and have a job and stuff like that. If you can't really change anything, what's the point?

Jean: I was called to do this, Stacy.

Stacy: Called? *(bewildered)* Who called you?

Jean: God called me. Jesus Christ called me.

Stacy: God? Jesus Christ? *(begins to get a little frustrated)* People are always saying that they were "called" by God. I just don't get this. I mean, I haven't had any experience with God yet that was that ... that ... *(struggles to find a word)* ... I don't know ... that "solid," I guess. When people talk about getting "called" by God it just seems too supernatural, too strange to be true. You have to wonder if people just make this stuff up. *(takes a deliberate breath. She is suddenly embarrassed)* I'm sorry ... I ... uh ... wasn't trying to say that I thought that you ... I mean ... I was just trying to understand some things. I was trying to ask you a simple question and now I'm babbling on like an idiot. Just forget it. I'm really sorry, okay?

Jean: *(gently, with a little laugh)* Stacy, it's okay. My relationship with God and his mission for me here on Earth is what I love to talk about the most! It's my purpose for living. And if you want to try to work out some things here with me tonight, I would be honored to help you with them. *(Jean looks for a response from Stacy, who says nothing. She is still very embarrassed. Jean continues)* I believe that what I am doing here is God's purpose for me. I never, ever planned on being here every day, feeding and comforting these people. One day, quite by accident, my path crossed with a homeless man who needed my help. I just knew what I had to do. I just knew that there was no other way I could act. From that moment on, the moment I truly decided to give my life to God and answer His call, things started happening so fast. It was like a downhill snowball going out of control ... a real chain reaction. *(pauses, then continues)* At times, I've been terrified. I was spending time in places many people never go. I was seeing things that many people never see. At times, I've felt like the whole thing was too overwhelming. I've even tried to tell God that this was too much for me, that He'd chosen the wrong person for His work.

Stacy: *(looking up at Jean now, realizing that she is not alone in her feelings)* Do you think God ever does that ... you know, choose the wrong person for the job? I mean, how does He decide who to ... uh ... you know ... "call"?

Jean: He is always calling all of us, Stacy. He doesn't pick who to call. He just patiently waits for us to hear Him. He starts on the day we begin life and continues even unto death. We just have to stop listening to all the "noise" of life and answer Him.

Stacy: The "noise" of life? What do you mean?

Jean: The "noise" of life is the stuff that we try to lie to ourselves about; the stuff we try to justify and defend; the things we try to make important that have nothing to do with our purpose in life. We must stop listening to all of the "noise" in life in order to be able to hear God calling us, and to answer that call.

Stacy: But what if you can't cut it? And how do you know what direction He wants you to take? And what about when you get scared? I thought that getting closer to God would always make me feel ... you know ... happier somehow.

Jean: I'm not pretending to have all the answers, but I do know that those times when you have doubts are the times when you aren't listening to God anymore ... when you try to lie to yourself about your beliefs. Being a Christian is hard work. It's not something you can do only on Sundays or Christmas or Easter. It's not good works or reciting passages from the Bible. Those things aren't enough. When you're sincere and really ready to follow Jesus' path, you'll find that your life changes immediately and, often times, pretty drastically.

Stacy: But how will I know when I'm ready for all that? I mean, how will I know when I've started to be a *real* Christian? Why now? Why like this? This seems like a strange way to be called by

God. It just doesn't seem like the way He would normally try to get through to people.

Jean: C'mon, Stacy, why are you making so many excuses? What's normal for God? A burning bush? The parting of the Red Sea? Maybe you were expecting a horrible tragedy like a plague or a flood?

Stacy: *(smiling weakly)* Well, the thought had kind of crossed my mind. What's so wrong with wanting some sort of sign? Some sort of proof?

Jean: Open your eyes, Stacy. The fact that you had a conversation with God to ask for a sign should be proof enough in itself. You were already *talking* to God. You already knew in your heart what was the truth ... that He exists. He didn't need to give you a "solid" sign as you call it. *We're* supposed to follow *His* Will; not the other way around. The way I see it, all of life is God's sign to us. Really look around you sometime, Stacy. Really look closely ... at the tiniest puff of dust under a microscope to the infinity of outer space. How can anyone possibly believe that this was all some sort of accident? How can any person experience the amazing connection of "coincidences" in their own lives and not believe in any purpose to it? No, Stacy, God is giving you signs every moment of every day. He's just waiting for you to open up your eyes and really see them.

Stacy: I know He exists. It's not that. I just think there could have been another way to get through to me.

Jean: You know, it's funny ... some people only talk to God when they have a terrible tragedy in their lives — for a lot of people, the first time they really try to talk to God is when someone close to them dies or when they are dying themselves. I always think that is the saddest thing in the world. Jesus Christ wants to be the best friend you ever had. ... a friend who gave his life for yours ... a friend who will always love you no matter how many times you turn your back on him ... a friend who already knows what you are thinking and feeling. You'll never feel compelled to lie to this friend because he already knows all the truths about you. He is willing to be there for you through the best and worst of your life and he asks so little of us in return. The way I see it, especially by today's standards, it's the deal of a lifetime.

Stacy: I never thought of Jesus as a friend before. I guess I'm just kind of worried about what he asks of us in return. I don't know if I can live up to that. I'm not too sure what he really wants from us anyway.

Jean: Jesus told us a commandment: "Love one another as I have loved you." It might not always be an easy thing to do, but if you really think about it, it *is* an easy thing to understand. It's pretty clear. "Love one another as I have loved you." Try to live by this. Let the Love of God into your heart and the rest will fall in place. You have to trust in God's love. It's called faith.

Stacy: But what happens when you fail? When you don't trust Him?

Jean: Usually, with me, that's when I feel angry, when I feel like God's not listening to me. He *always* calls me back. He *always* gives me an answer.

Stacy: He *always* gives you an answer?

Jean: *Always* ... and He always forgives me and He always welcomes me back when I return from letting my faith weaken. But being a Christian isn't easy. It's just like me here, helping these people. You're right, I do get frustrated at times. I wonder if I'm really making any sort of difference. Then, usually in the most unlikely of places, I find out that I *am* making a difference, that God's will did win out over the temptations, the "noise," we have here on Earth. I can't fully describe it, Stacy, but complete faith in God is the best feeling there is.

Stacy: *(sadly)* I guess I'll have to take your word for it. I'm afraid I wasn't very successful at following God's will.

Jean: Don't feel too badly. You may find God will surprise you. His presence can be a very powerful thing. Some believe that no single moment in life happens by accident — that there's a reason you are here with me now ... *(almost whispers)* Open your eyes. Shut out the "noise" of life, Stacy, and listen closely to what God is telling you. He'll help you find your purpose. You'll have your answers.

(They are interrupted by loud party music ... laughing and dancing. A group of teens enter, arms full — with lights, food, boxes of clothing, shoes, blankets, toiletries, firewood, and so forth.)

Carmen: *(leading a conga line of teens carrying boxes, and so forth)* Okay, that's great, you guys. Just put that stuff down anywhere until we figure out what to do with it. *(turns to Stacy with a big grin)* Well, Stacy, you wouldn't come to the party, so we brought the party to you!

Stacy: *(shocked, embarrassed, with eyes wide)* Carmen, I really don't think this is the place for this ... *(nervously taking her aside)* I mean, I signed up for this at church. Can't you guys find another place?

Carmen: *(laughing)* Don't worry, Stacy. I've got everything under control, okay. Hey, Ms. Jean, you don't care if we give away these shoes, blankets, and food, do you?

Jean: *(pleasantly surprised)* Why, no ... no, of course not! Here, let me help you.

(Jean busies herself with the teens and their boxes. She starts to help them distribute the items to the people at the shelter. Stacy is shocked. With jaw open, she turns to a beaming Carmen.)

Stacy: Carmen, what is all of this? What are you doing here? What happened to your party?

Carmen: This *is* my party! *(softer, more seriously)* Look, Stacy, I wore that bracelet you gave me. I planned to lie if anyone asked me about the "W.W.J.D." I planned to stick with my Wild Women of Jefferson Drive routine. After all, I figured no one knew what it really meant anyway. It should've been easy ...

Stacy: And?

Carmen: And it wasn't so easy. I knew what it really meant and I just couldn't bring myself to lie about something so ... *(struggles to find the word)* ... so ... I don't know ... so religious. I started to play it off when Sarah asked me about it, but I couldn't. I ended up telling her all about it. We started thinking about you ... you know, down here feeding the homeless instead of going to the party. Well, anyway, after that, we tried to just forget about it and get into the party and all ... *(trails off)*

Stacy: And?

Carmen: And I just couldn't get into it. No matter how hard I tried, I just kept having this feeling that I was missing something ... this really funny feeling that wouldn't go away. I found Sarah again and told her how I kept having this funny feeling, and she said she did, too ... ever since we talked about the bracelet and you being down here. We even tried to laugh it off. You know, blame it on the salsa dip or something, but it was like we were both thinking the same thing. So, we decided to make up a couple of care packages — just a couple of bags of stuff from the party food, and grab a couple of old blankets, and come down here to see if we could help you out or anything.

Stacy: Okay, Carmen, that explains you and Sarah, but what are all the rest of these people doing here? This must be half the people at your party! And that's definitely more stuff than blankets and party food.

Carmen: Well, that's the really strange part. I mean, you just can't imagine how the smallest little thing, a good thing, can have such an amazing chain reaction!

Stacy: Oh, I don't know ... try me. *(glances to the spot on her wrist where her bracelet used to be)*

Carmen: Well, Sarah and I weren't planning on telling anyone else about all of this, but when we started loading the stuff in Sarah's car, people started asking all of these questions.

Stacy: *(smiling to herself)* Imagine that! *(to Carmen)* And? What did you tell them?

Carmen: And I told them the truth — that I felt like this was something I needed to do — that these people needed us more than we needed another party. I thought everyone would laugh and think we were crazy, but ... *(stops, teasing Stacy now, saving up to tell her the most amazing part)*

Stacy: *(after waiting for Carmen to finish, Stacy prompts, almost screaming)* BUT WHAT?!?!?!?!? C'mon, Carmen. You can't stop there!

Carmen: *(delighted — the words bubble out. She couldn't wait to tell it anyway)* But instead of laughing, the next thing I know someone yells out that everyone could go grab an old pair of shoes, and someone else says they'll get blankets, and then all these people start to talk at once, everybody with new ideas that just keep getting better and better, and before you know it we've got like this line of cars all loaded up and ready to go. It was really strange. It was like I had this one little idea and pretty soon it caught on and everyone was thinking the same thing ... like some sort of ... I don't know ...

Stacy: *(interrupting her)* Like some sort of downhill snowball growing larger and faster as it goes?

Carmen: Exactly! Stacy! I'm so glad you understand. I was worried you might be mad or like embarrassed or something that we all came down here and all. I mean, it was just like something else had gotten control of things.

Stacy: Mad at you? Carmen, this is great! I mean, I can't believe you guys did all of this! I mean, this is unbelievable!

Carmen: *(hesitantly)* Stacy, that's not all. It gets even more unbelievable ...

Stacy: *(speaks up to sky, almost as if she were addressing God again. She speaks as she sits)* I have a feeling I might want to sit down for this one.

Carmen: *(after a pause)* When it eventually came out what the "W.W.J.D." on my bracelet really meant and how it started the whole thing, well, I mean, everybody was running around all excited getting stuff together and they just all start saying, "I want one. Yeah, me too. Me too!" you know? So, the next thing I know somebody's got a magic marker and paper and they're all making these bracelets and putting them on. Some of the really psyched up ones even started writing it on their skin instead of waiting for the paper. I just needed to tell you about it. I didn't want you to think they were trying to make fun of you or your bracelet or anything. I mean, look at this, Stacy. Isn't this amazing?

(They turn together. With backs to the audience, they look at the group. At the moment Carmen says "amazing," everyone must freeze in position. Stacy turns to the audience to address God again as in Act I. This conversation is really happening in her mind as she watches the group. When she finishes her speech, she will turn back to the spot she was in when Carmen said "amazing" and everyone froze. The group will unfreeze and continue action as if nothing had happened.)

Stacy: Hello? God? Okay, Carmen's right, this *is* pretty amazing. Um ... I don't know ... what can I say? *(smiles)* I think I get it now! Heh! Heh! *(pauses, frowns and gets serious)* About the last time we talked ... I'm sorry. I said a lot of things that I shouldn't have said. I don't need a plague or flood or anything like that. You can hang on to those if You'd like and it would be just fine with me, okay? I guess I was so busy asking You for things that I didn't hear You calling me. I really am sorry that I walked away when You were trying to be my friend. I know how much that hurts ... *(pauses)* I really do. God, what You did here today, with all of these people, I just want to say thank you. I mean, I basically spit in your face and then You let something really amazing and wonderful like this happen. Thank you. I mean, I'm going to try to be a better friend back, okay? God, I don't know if You noticed ... *(looks around the frozen group)* ... but Jan isn't here ... *(pauses and then says sadly)* She must have stayed at the party with Darrell. Well, God, I know I don't have any place to ask You for anything, but I love Jan. I mean, she and I have been best friends since we were babies. God, I'm asking You to look after her tonight, please. I'm not asking this for myself. I'm really worried about her. Please? I have this feeling that something's going to happen to her tonight that will change her life forever. Just help her, okay? Please? *(pauses and thinks)* God, I know I have Your love in my heart now. I'm going to try to have faith, too. I will trust You.

(Stacy and Carmen become part of the animated group, people showing their bracelets and the stuff they brought with them. Jan and Darrell enter quietly from the side and stand, arm-in-arm, looking very much in love, smiling at each other. Jan catches Stacy's eye from across the room and waves. Stacy deliberately turns away and walks to the other side of the room, as far away from Jan as she can get. She turns her back to Jan. Jan whispers something to Darrell. Darrell looks at Stacy, nods, gives Jan a kiss, and joins the others. Jan walks over to Stacy.)

Jan: Stacy, we have to talk ... okay? *(Stacy doesn't respond)* Stacy, something happened tonight that has probably changed my whole life and I want to tell my best friend about it.

Stacy: *(with a deep breath)* Look, Jan, I don't want to hear any details, okay? You know how I feel. Nothing has changed about that. And, Jan, I think you made it perfectly clear how you felt about my opinion. Remember, Jan? You didn't want my weird Jesus bracelet when you knew what the letters on it meant. You wanted me to just leave you alone. Well, don't worry, Jan. My stupid little bracelet won't have to bother you anymore because I threw it away anyway.

Jan: I don't understand ... You threw it away?

Stacy: Yeah, I threw it away. I know it was a stupid thing to do. I should have saved it. After all, it was a gift from my grandmother. It's just that ... at the time, I guess I thought they were made to be given away and if I couldn't even get my best friend to take one from me ... well, then I figured I probably didn't deserve to have it anyway. Don't worry, Jan. It's not your fault. I mean, look at this ... *(motions toward the people behind them)* ... this is craziness! I probably think too much about stuff. You go and have your dream life with Darrell and leave me to drive myself crazy trying to make sense of it all.

Jan: Oh ... well, then I guess you'll need this. *(holds out the bracelet on her arm)*

Stacy: *(surprised and confused)* What's that? Jan, how did you get that? That's my bracelet!

Jan: *(smiling)* I thought you threw it away.

Stacy: I did. But how did you get it?

Jan: You know that day you first tried to give it to me? Well, I went back to talk to you. You know, to try to work things out. I mean, we never really fought before. I just couldn't leave it like that. I had decided that you were my best friend, and if you really wanted me to wear the bracelet then I would wear it — no matter how uncomfortable it made me feel. When I got there, you were gone and I found the bracelet on the ground. I didn't want you to lose it, so I put it on and it's been there ever since. I wanted to be able to give it to you as soon as I saw you again, so I just never took it off.

Stacy: You wore it to the party?

Jan: Yes, I wore it to the party. Stacy, that's what I'm trying to tell you. I was scared — really scared. Look, Stacy, nothing happened — at least not what you think! I love Darrell, but there's so many questions and things to consider. *(pauses and then continues softly)* Stacy, I ended up telling Darrell how scared I was and nervous and he told me he was nervous and a little scared. And then there was your bracelet, staring me in the face. I just kept seeing those letters — "What Would Jesus Do?" "What Would Jesus Do?" *(long pause)* So, I told Darrell about the bracelet and what it meant. I was so scared. I thought he would think I was some sort of strange geek and dump me for sure.

Stacy: Well, by the looks of things, I can see that he didn't dump you.

Jan: No, it was like he was looking for a place to find some answers, too. The more we talked about it, the less scared and confused we got. The more we talked about it, the closer we became. Stacy, I was angry at you because I thought you were trying to give me something to come *between* Darrell and me. It turned out to be something that brought us even closer together. Stacy, we've decided to wait — you know — wait until we both have a clearer idea of what our purpose is in life. Darrell's never even been in a church in his whole life, but he likes to read and he said that he always did have to admit that Jesus was one of the most significant people in history and his impact on the modern world couldn't be compared with anyone else. Darrell said he could see how this would be a good person to choose as a role model — infinitely better than people like Mike Tyson and Dennis Rodman. He said he wants to start reading more about Jesus' life so he can understand his teachings better and find some answers to his own questions and confusion.

Stacy: Wait a minute! Darrell's *never* been to church and now he wants to read the Bible? I don't believe it!

Jan: Pretty amazing, huh? I can't describe it, Stacy. It was like once I decided to let Jesus guide me to the answers to my questions, it lifted some sort of load off my shoulders. I don't know what it's called, but I've never felt better, less confused.

Stacy: I think I know what it's called. It's called faith. It means that you trust that "What Jesus Would Do" is the right decision. It means that you trust God and put your life in His hands. It means that everyday — not just on Sundays and holidays — you need to live every minute always thinking "What Would Jesus Do?" *(long pause)* Yeah, Jan, you're right. I *do* want my bracelet back to help me remember what faith is all about. But what about you? Don't you want a bracelet, too?

Jan: That's why Darrell and I were so late getting here. You said your grandmother sent you home with a big suitcase full of "W.W.J.D" bracelets, so we stopped by your house and asked your mom for them before we came here. I hope you don't mind. We already put ours on. *(Darrell joins them)*

Stacy: What are you going to do with the rest of them?

Jan: Oh, I don't know. It just seems like once people hear about them, they want one sooner or later, either for themselves or someone else. You know everybody needs a reminder now and then that our lives are a gift from God, that we owe it to Him to think about His will before we act.

Carmen: You know, Stacy, we've all been talking and we came up with a whole list of things that would change in the world if people would just start asking themselves, "What Would Jesus Do?"

Stacy: What kind of things?

(The kids start to throw out all kinds of ideas. Assign lines and comments to those who want them.)

Teens: A whole list.
It's endless.
Think about it.
Violence.
What Would Jesus Do?
Teen pregnancy.
What Would Jesus Do?
Drugs.
Politics.
Hunger.
Terrorism.
Homelessness.
Racism.
Discrimination.
Child abuse and neglect.
War.
Pollution.
Corporate greed.
Animal suffering.
Respect for human life.

Carmen: Just thinking, "What Would Jesus Do?" would eliminate so many terrible things in the world ... even simple things could make a big difference.

Teens: Yeah, stuff like gossiping.
Littering.
Reckless driving.
Respecting your parents and family.
Teasing other people.
Drunken driving.
Using offensive language.
Lying.
Shoplifting.
Flipping someone off on the highway.
You really have to think What Would Jesus Do?
If this could catch on, the differences would be tremendous.
People would smile more.
They'd help each other.
Churches would be full,
and prisons would be empty — not the other way around.

Stacy: I know, I understand now how one person can start a chain reaction. One person can make a difference, but I still don't know of anyone who might be interested in having some of these bracelets. *(turns to the congregation)* Yet, somehow, I feel like ... maybe ... just maybe if we each took some of these and we each took its message with us and we started walking straight ahead, I just feel like maybe we will find some arms outstretched, just waiting to be the next link in our "What Would Jesus Do?" chain reaction.

(The cast holds out their arms to show the congregation and begins distributing two bracelets from a suitcase to each person present, on stage and off. If no one in the congregation holds out their arms for the bracelets, the cast should ask politely.)

www.ingramcontent.com/pod-product-compliance
Lightning Source LLC
Chambersburg PA
CBHW071751020426
42331CB00008B/2275